DANIEL BOULUD

MIXOLOGIST XAVIER HERIT

Cocktails

& AMUSE-BOUCHES

For Him

Slipcase front: Xavier Herit's The Duke.
Slipcase back: Detail of the bar at Daniel,
photograph by Cécilia Maurin and Damion Tedeschi.
Endpapers: The bar at Daniel.

All other photographs by Harald Gottschalk.
Illustrations by Rafael Alterio.

All glassware by Riedel.

© The Dinex Group
© 2011 Assouline Publishing
601 West 26th Street, 18th floor
New York, NY 10001, USA
Tel.: 212-989-6810   Fax: 212-647-0005
www.assouline.com
Printed in China.
ISBN: 978 1 61428 002 6
Design by Camille Dubois.

DANIEL BOULUD

MIXOLOGIST XAVIER HERIT

Cocktails
& AMUSE-BOUCHES

For Him

ASSOULINE

Cocktails

Amuse-Bouches

Foreword by Jay McInerney

The Upper East Side of Manhattan is one of the world's grand urban neighborhoods, an Olympian refuge for the wealthy and powerful, a realm of exclusive prewar co-operative apartment buildings guarded by liveried doormen, from which exceptionally well-dressed women occasionally emerge to make brief appearances on the public space of the sidewalk before ducking into waiting black town cars. It's not a world that offers many portals to outsiders, but if you wanted to feel like a native, and to observe them in their natural habitat, you would be well advised to take a seat at the bar at Daniel, on East 65th Street, just off Park Avenue. Order a cocktail. After you've downed a French 65 or The Duke, you'll start to feel at home. This is what a great bar is for, to serve as a temporary refuge from the world outside and to make you feel, for as long as you sit and sip, that you are an insider, a member of a small, exclusive club—although there are few bars as chic and as beautiful as this one, and there aren't many bartenders as innovative as Xavier Herit. He reinvents the standards of American mixology in much the same way that Daniel Boulud reinterprets the great classics of French cuisine. Herit's creations often have a sense of whimsy, like the maple syrup in his New Fashioned old fashioned, without seeming to indulge novelty for its own sake. Have another—maybe the Basil Haven, a new-wave martini. Relax. Check out the scenery: that very attractive woman in the little black dress just across the lounge, for instance, the one who ordered the East Side Bellini—from the Hers side of the His and Hers cocktail menu, naturally. The night is just beginning.

Introduction by Daniel Boulud

There is an art to making a good cocktail. The person who prepares it must have a good palate, a good sense of ingredients, and the ability to combine them by playing with the savory, the sweet, and the tart.

In France, we don't usually drink cocktails. There, we drink wine with meals, and spirits are taken straight up, or with a little water perhaps, like Pernod or pastis, or whiskey. I didn't discover cocktails until I arrived in New York, with my first memorable sip at the old Trader Vic's, the famed tiki bar at the Plaza Hotel.

In the last decade, cocktails have truly morphed into more original creations, reaching far beyond the basics. Chefs are becoming involved with the bar, and bartenders are becoming involved with the kitchen, creating a wonderful synergy between these once separate restaurant realms. Like me, bartender Xavier Herit is French: He does not come from a culture of cocktails, but the discovery of this aspect of the culinary world has been an exciting journey around the globe for him, just as it is for me.

I see cocktails today as a gastronomic element as creative, complex, and original as cooking. Not everything works, of course; it's about balance. You don't want to feel the excess of any one ingredient, be it alcohol, acidity, sweetness, or spice. The perfect cocktail is one in which each element can be discerned but none overpowers another, and Xavier understands this very well.

Xavier and I also understand each other's palates, and there is a good trust between us. As with my chefs in the kitchen, I talk and exchange ideas about the bar with him. For instance, when he was first working on the recipe for the fantastic Jaipur Sour (page 26), I showed him the spice rack in the kitchen and pointed out the colorful sugar-coated fennel seeds that are used in Indian cuisine to cleanse the palate after a meal. He found them utterly fascinating, and became inspired to use them as the perfect garnish on that cocktail, so full of exotic, interesting flavor, translating a culinary practice into mixology.

I have always put an emphasis on good cocktails at Daniel, although it's not a public bar and we don't promote it that way. (But it is one of New York's best-kept secrets.) Our guests have the privilege of amazing service, and well-trained professionals like Xavier, presented in a beautiful setting. While you may not be able to re-create the experience of Daniel, you can keep these same elements in mind when you host a gathering, using Xavier's cocktails and my special small-bite recipes—many of which can be made beforehand, and even frozen, to help you stay organized—to create a perfectly entertaining evening at home.

As for the cocktails, my advice is to be sure to always measure your ingredients (Xavier does!) and keep good-quality liquor on hand. Use fresh, seasonal ingredients whenever possible, and while I encourage you to be creative, remember that the drinks that become classics aren't about smoke and mirrors or excess of presentation—they're about great combinations.

To your health!

Cocktails

The Duke

1	1 oz Pierre Ferrand 1er Cru du Cognac
2	1 oz Amaro Montenegro
3	1 oz Carpano Antica Formula vermouth
4	2 drops The Bitter Truth orange bitters
5	1 orange peel

In a mixing glass, stir together cognac, amaro, vermouth, and orange bitters with ice. Strain into a large, hollow ice ball* placed in a rocks glass. Garnish with orange peel.

Making a triumphant return to the cocktail landscape is the Negroni, with a tempting red hue and a bitter-fruity nature that whets the palate. I replace gin with cognac, and served in a rock, not on the rocks, it looks like a beautiful heart.

* See Supplemental Recipes.

First Word

1 | ¾ oz Blue Gin

2 | ¾ oz green Chartreuse

3 | ¾ oz St-Germain elderflower liqueur

4 | ¾ oz lime juice

5 | 1 lime peel

In a shaker, combine liquid ingredients with ice. Shake and strain into a chilled martini or stem glass and garnish with lime twist.

The pre-Prohibition era truly was the first word
in cocktails. This play on the old Detroit Athletic
Club uses my favorite gin, Blue Gin from Austria,
with notes of flowers, spice, and herbs.
With lime juice and herby green Chartreuse,
this is the perfect refreshment.

Bitter for Better

This twist substitutes aged Venezuelan rum and a combination of bitters for a sophisticated balance.

1 | 2 oz Santa Teresa 1796 rum

2 | 1 oz Bonal Gentiane-Quina

3 | 4 drops Angostura bitters

4 | 4 drops Peychaud's bitters

5 | rinse of Fernet-Branca

6 | 1 orange peel

When I first moved to New York, drinks were on the sweet side, but now more savory and bitter-based classics like the Manhattan have become popular again.

In a mixing glass, stir together rum, Bonal, and both bitters with ice. Rinse a rocks glass with Fernet-Branca, discard, and add a 2"-square ice cube. Strain mixture into glass and garnish with orange peel.

El Hombre

1   2 oz Herradura Silver tequila

2   1 oz Cointreau

3   1 oz cucumber juice*

4   ½ oz lime juice

5   6-8 sprigs cilantro

6   ½ piece dried Thai chili pepper

7   1 tsp Sugar in the Raw

8   1 whole dried Thai chili

9   1 cilantro leaf

There is so much more to tequila than people realize. Herradura Silver with muddled fresh cilantro and raw sugar (the grains help the muddling process), a little Thai chili, and smooth cucumber juice makes a margarita for the modern age.

In a shaker, muddle lime juice, cilantro sprigs, ½ piece of Thai chili, and sugar. Add tequila, Cointreau, cucumber juice, and ice. Shake vigorously and double strain into ice-filled glass. Garnish with cilantro leaf and whole Thai chili.

* See Supplemental Recipes.

Golden Lion

1	2 oz Pyrat XO rum
2	¾ oz Marie Brizard orange Curaçao
3	1 oz club soda
4	½ oz lime juice
5	¼ oz simple syrup*
6	¼ oz ginger juice*
7	1 piece candied ginger

I call this the Golden Lion because its color seems to glow from the golden Guyana rum, and the spicy, fresh ginger juice roars on your tongue. The orange Curaçao gives body and the lime juice keeps the flavors balanced and focused.

In a shaker, combine liquid ingredients with ice. Shake and strain into an ice-filled highball glass. Garnish with piece of candied ginger.

* See Supplemental Recipes.

20

Virgin Mojito

1   2 oz ginger ale

2   2 oz club soda

3   ½ oz lime juice

4   ½ oz simple syrup*

5   5–8 mint leaves

6   1 tsp Sugar in the Raw

7   1 lime slice

Why should alcohol imbibers have all the fun? The popular mojito doesn't have to include white rum; it's really about the refreshing mint and lime. Top it off with club soda and ginger ale for a sophisticated mocktail worthy of any occasion.

Muddle lime juice, simple syrup, mint leaves, and sugar in a highball glass. Add ice, ginger ale, and club soda, and stir. Garnish with slice of lime and mint leaf.

* See Supplemental Recipes.

Dr. Stormy

This is a play on the Dark and Stormy,
a simple combination of rum and ginger beer.

1   2 oz lapsang souchong tea–infused cognac*

2   2 oz homemade ginger beer*

3   ½ oz lemon juice

4   ½ oz simple syrup*

5   1 piece candied ginger

I infuse cognac with smoky lapsang souchong tea, which almost tastes like a peaty Scotch. With house-made ginger beer, it's just what the doctor ordered.

In a shaker, combine cognac, lemon juice, and simple syrup with ice. Shake and strain into an ice-filled glass. Add ginger beer using a soda siphon, and garnish with piece of candied ginger.

* See Supplemental Recipes.

Jaipur Sour

1 | 2 oz Tanqueray No. Ten gin

2 | ¾ oz Rothman & Winter Orchard Apricot liqueur

3 | ½ oz lemon juice

4 | ¼ oz simple syrup*

5 | 1 sprig curry leaves

6 | 1 espresso spoon Sugar in the Raw

7 | Candied fennel seeds

Fresh curry leaves have a more toasted aroma than when dried and powdered. Muddled with brown sugar and lemon juice, their flavor becomes delicate and pretty, and goes incredibly well with gin's citrusy notes. Add a little apricot liqueur and candied fennel seeds for an Indian-influenced drink.

In a shaker, muddle curry leaves with sugar and lemon juice. Add gin, apricot liqueur, and simple syrup, and shake together with ice. Strain into a rocks glass with a 2"-square ice cube. Garnish with a curry leaf and candied fennel seeds on top of the ice.

* See Supplemental Recipes.

French 6₅

1	3 oz Champagne
2	1 oz Cointreau
3	6 drops Angostura bitters
4	1 orange peel

In a mixing glass, combine Cointreau and bitters with ice and stir. Strain into a frozen Champagne glass and add Champagne. Spritz the cocktail with an orange twist.

This drink is a play on the French 75 and an address--ours.
Restaurant Daniel is on 65th Street, and since Daniel are I French…
For my version of this classic, I substitute Cointreau for
cognac to let the aromas dazzle when mixed with the Champagne.

Batida de Coco and Kaffir

1 | 2 oz oolong tea–infused Leblon cachaça*

2 | 1 oz coconut milk

3 | ¾ oz simple syrup*

4 | ½ oz lime juice

5 | 1 kaffir lime leaf

In a shaker, combine liquid ingredients with ice. Shake vigorously and strain into an ice-filled rocks glass. Garnish with kaffir lime leaf.

Cachaça infused with oolong tea mimics the deep aroma of cognac, and kaffir lime leaves brighten up tropical coconut milk. In Portuguese, *batida* means shaken, or milkshake, which is what the pale color and frothy texture of this drink remind me of.

* See Supplemental Recipes.

Bourbon T' Sour

1 | 2 oz Earl Grey tea–infused
    Wild Turkey 101-proof bourbon*

2 | 1 oz lemon juice

3 | ¾ oz simple syrup*

4 | 4 drops Angostura bitters

5 | 3 brandied cherries

6 | 1 lemon peel

I went through a phase of drinking Earl Grey tea with breakfast, and I realized that its bergamot aroma would play well with the vanilla notes in bourbon.

In a shaker, combine liquid ingredients with ice. Shake and strain into a martini glass. Garnish with brandied cherries and lemon peel.

* See Supplemental Recipes.

Pumpkin Smash

1	1½ oz Appleton Estate V/X rum
2	¾ oz spice syrup*
3	½ oz lemon juice
4	½ oz pumpkin puree
5	1 drop The Bitter Truth Jerry Thomas' Own Decanter bitters
6	1 cinnamon stick
7	3 cloves

Seasonal flavors play a big role in my cocktails, and inspired by Thanksgiving, I blended pumpkin puree with house-made spice syrup, a drop of Bitter Truth, lemon juice, and rich Jamaican aged rum. It's like sipping autumn.

In a shaker, combine liquid ingredients with ice. Shake and strain into a rocks glass with a 2"-square ice cube. Garnish with cinnamon stick and cloves.

* See Supplemental Recipes.

Basil Haven

Folklore holds that Indonesian cubeb peppers are a cure-all, for everything from bad breath to fever.

1 | 2 oz Hendrick's gin

2 | ¾ oz St-Germain elderflower liqueur

3 | 1 oz cucumber juice*

4 | ½ oz lime juice

5 | 1 tsp Sugar in the Raw

6 | 1 sprig basil leaves

7 | 10 Indonesian cubeb peppercorns

I can't promise this drink will fix what ails you, but Hendrick's gin, elderflower liqueur, cucumber and lime juices, and basil marry well with the mildly bitter cubeb.

In a shaker top, muddle lime juice, sugar, basil sprig, and cubeb peppercorns. Add gin, elderflower liqueur, and cucumber juice, and shake together with ice. Double strain into chilled martini glass. Float basil leaf with cubeb peppercorns as garnish.

* See Supplemental Recipes.

Pomp and Circumstance

1 | 2 oz Blue Gin

2 | ½ oz green Chartreuse

3 | 1 oz grapefruit juice

4 | 1 oz club soda

5 | ½ oz lemon juice

6 | ½ oz simple syrup*

7 | 1 grapefruit peel

This isn't about serious occasions, it's based on a play on words. I was making a cocktail using pink grapefruit--it was summer, around the time that schools hold graduation ceremonies. The French word for grapefruit is *pamplemousse*, which sounds like the famed graduation song.

In a shaker, combine gin, Chartreuse, grapefruit juice, lemon juice, and simple syrup with ice. Shake and strain into an ice-filled highball glass and top with club soda. Garnish with grapefruit peel.

* See Supplemental Recipes.

New Fashioned

1   1½ oz Rittenhouse 100-proof rye

2   ¾ oz Carpano Punt e Mes vermouth

3   ¼ oz McLure's maple syrup

4   8 drops Fee Brothers peach bitters

5   4 drops Peychaud's bitters

6   1 orange peel

7   1 lemon peel

The cocktail renaissance has revived many great classics, including rare ingredients and spirits like the wonderfully herby rye whiskey. I created this version of the old fashioned with a nearly forgotten bittersweet Italian vermouth and maple syrup.

In a mixing glass, stir together rye, vermouth, maple syrup, and both bitters with ice. Strain into a rocks glass with a large ice ball. Garnish with lemon and orange peels.

Mayfair Sour

I had to name a drink after our building, Mayfair House,
first a hotel and now a residential building.

1 | 1 oz Plymouth gin

2 | ¾ oz Benedictine

3 | ¾ oz apricot liqueur

4 | ¾ oz lemon juice

5 | 1 egg white

6 | 5 drops peach bitters

Made with Plymouth
gin, Benedictine,
lemon juice, and
apricot liqueur,
it feels like a drop
of apricot nectar
on your tongue.

In a shaker, combine all ingredients except bitters and shake once without ice, then shake again with ice. Strain into a chilled martini glass. For garnish, dash a few drops of bitters on top of foam.

My Tie

1 1 oz Clément Première Canne rum

2 1 oz Appleton Estate V/X rum

3 ½ oz Marie Brizard orange Curaçao

4 ¾ oz almond syrup

5 ¾ oz lime juice

6 1 orange peel

7 1 lime peel

In a shaker, combine liquid ingredients with ice. Shake and strain into a highball glass filled with crushed ice. Garnish with orange and lime peels combined into a geometric decoration.

Smokey Bandit

1 | 1½ oz Ilegal Mezcal Joven

2 | ¾ oz Marie Brizard orange Curaçao

3 | 1 oz pineapple juice

4 | ½ oz lime juice

5 | ¼ oz simple syrup*

6 | 8 drops jalapeño juice*

7 | 1 jalapeño slice

Mescal has made a big impact on my recipes, because it adds intense complexity. With sweet pineapple to balance the kick of jalapeño, orange Curaçao and lime juice for body, the surprising, smoky mescal sneaks up on your palate like a bandit.

In a shaker, combine liquid ingredients with ice. Shake and strain into a rocks glass with a 2"-square ice cube. Garnish with thin slice of jalapeño on top of ice cube.

* See Supplemental Recipes.

Irish Pear

1 | 2 oz Jameson Irish whiskey

2 | 1 oz pear puree

3 | ½ oz lemon juice

4 | ½ oz cinnamon syrup*

5 | 2 thin pear slices

In a shaker, combine liquid ingredients with ice. Shake and strain into a chilled martini glass. Garnish with two slices of pear on the rim of the glass.

Irish whiskey is so soft and easygoing, it makes a great complement with pear puree. The addition of house-crafted cinnamon syrup--water and sugar gently simmered with cinnamon sticks--makes this a perfect warming drink for fall.

* See Supplemental Recipes.

The Revolutionary

1	1½ oz Woodford Reserve bourbon
2	1 oz white crème de menthe
3	¾ oz white crème de cacao
4	rinse of absinthe
5	1 lemon twist

In a mixing glass, combine bourbon, crème de menthe, and crème de cacao with ice and stir. Rinse an old fashioned glass with absinthe, add a 2"-square ice cube, and strain in contents of mixing glass. Garnish with lemon twist.

I wanted an after-dinner drink that wasn't too sweet, and created a cross between a Sazerac and a Stinger. Refreshing but complex, with beauty and strength, sweetness, herbiness, and a lemony kick, the mix of complementary flavors represents the revolution in cocktail culture.

Amuse-Bouches

Shiso-Ponzu
Fluke (Makes approximately 25-40)

Cut 2 fillets of skinless, boneless fluke
lengthwise into 1" batons and place in a
shallow, non-reactive container.

In a small bowl, combine ½ cup ponzu sauce
with the juice and zest of one lime.
Pour over the fluke, and refrigerate
for 2 hours, turning the fish every
½ hour for even marinating.

Meanwhile, shave a large daikon radish into very
thin slices with a mandoline, and trim the slices
into ½"-wide by 3"-long rectangles.
Set aside and keep moist.

Slice 3 small bunches of shiso into ½"-wide strips
from stem to tip. Remove fluke from marinade,
sprinkle generously with togarashi spice blend on
all sides, and then cut into bite-size cubes.

Top a rectangle of daikon with a strip of
shiso, and wrap around a cube of fish,
securing with a toothpick.

Repeat with all remaining fish
and serve immediately.

Yuzu Razor Clam Ceviche (Makes 24)

Remove 12 live razor clams from their shells
and trim, rinse, and slice them thinly.

Place the shells in a large pot,

cover with water,

and bring to a boil.

Drain, rinse, scrub, and trim the shells.

Season the sliced clams with 2 tbsp
Kewpie mayonnaise, ¼ cup
sliced scallions, and yuzu juice, salt,
and espelette pepper to taste.

Evenly distribute the seasoned clam mixture into

the shells, on one end,

like in a spoon.

Garnish with more
sliced scallions
and serve chilled.

Sweetbreads à la Diable

(Makes approximately 60)

Soak 2 lbs of sweetbreads in a large bowl of ice water in the refrigerator for 8 hours, changing water at least twice.

Transfer to a saucepan and cover with cold water and a pinch of salt. Bring to a boil, then simmer lightly for 5 minutes.

Strain and chill. Trim away any fat and tough connective tissue, then portion the sweetbreads into 1-2" morsels.

Place 1 cup flour, 3 whipped eggs, and 1 cup fine bread crumbs in separate shallow containers. Dust the sweetbreads in flour, then dip in egg, and dredge in bread crumbs.

When ready to serve,
deep-fry in 350° F vegetable oil
until golden brown, drain on
paper towel-lined plate,
and sprinkle with salt.

Serve with sauce diable for dipping.

        Sauce diable:
In a small bowl,
          combine 2 tbsp Dijon mustard,
      2 tsp Worcestershire sauce,
      ½ cup ketchup, 8 drops Tabasco,
      3 tbsp steak sauce,
and 2 tsp white wine vinegar.

Black Olive Grissini

Fill a piping bag with a ¼" tip
with black olive tapenade. Divide grissini
dough* in four and press flat.

With a pasta machine,
roll one piece of dough through the largest setting,
fold in thirds, and repeat twice.

Decrease width by one setting;
pass the dough through and repeat,
continuing to decrease
until the dough is
$1/_{16}$" thick and approximately
2' long by 5" wide.
Trim edges into straight lines.
Repeat with remaining 3 pieces of dough.

Brush two sheets of dough with water
and pipe three lines of tapenade
horizontally through the middle, leaving a
finger's width of space between lines.

Place remaining two sheets on top
and press lightly
between tapenade lines
and on edges; freeze.

Whip one egg with 1 tbsp water,
and brush on top of dough;
sprinkle with espelette pepper and fleur de sel.

Cut widthwise into $1/8$"-wide sticks
to expose the 3 pockets of tapenade;
transfer to parchment paper-lined baking
sheets, leaving $1/2$" of space between sticks.

Rest, covered,

in a warm spot for 30 minutes.

Bake at 360°F for 8 minutes,

rotate tray 180° and bake

another 4 minutes until

golden brown.

*See Supplemental Recipes.

Rio's Bolinho

Place 2 lbs hot,
        tender, boiled yucca root
in a food processor
            with 3 tbsp butter
and puree until smooth.

Transfer to a mixing bowl; check for

    and discard any fibrous threads.

Add 1 whipped egg,

  ½ cup manioc (yucca) flour,

1 tbsp chopped aromatic pickled

Brazilian peppers,

  2 tbsp chopped cilantro,

and salt and pepper to taste;

         stir until well combined.

         With floured hands,

roll mixture into 1"-diameter balls; chill.

  In separate shallow containers,

              place 1 cup flour,

     3 whipped eggs,

   and 1 cup fine bread crumbs.

Dust the balls in flour, dip in the egg,

     and dredge in bread crumbs.

   When ready to serve,

   deep-fry in 350° F vegetable oil

   until golden brown, strain onto a

       paper towel-lined plate,

and sprinkle with salt. Serve warm.

Squid and Chorizo

(Serves 16-20)

Clean 2 lbs of baby squid
      and cut the bodies into rings;
Place in a bowl, cover with milk,
    and soak overnight in refrigerator.

In a small skillet over medium heat,
crisp ½ cup finely diced chorizo
in 1/3 cup olive oil.

Using a slotted spoon,
      transfer chorizo onto paper towels
      and reserve the oil.

In a medium bowl,
      whisk together 1 egg yolk,
            1 finely grated clove of garlic,
            the juice of 1 lemon,
      and a pinch of salt and pepper.

Using a whisk to emulsify,
      slowly stream in the reserved chorizo oil
            and then ½ cup grapeseed oil
      to reach the consistency
            of a thick mayonnaise.
Adjust seasoning with more salt
            and Tabasco sauce, if desired.

Drain squid and pat dry.
Combine 1/3 cup Wondra flour
and ¼ cup cornstarch in a bowl
with a sprinkle of salt and pepper.

      Dust squid in flour mixture, shake off excess,
            and when ready to serve,
            deep-fry in 350°F vegetable oil
                  for 20-30 seconds,
      until crispy and golden.

Serve with chorizo mayonnaise
with crisped chorizo sprinkled on top.

Sardines and Seaweed Butter on Puffed Rice Cracker

(Serves approximately 40)

In a small bowl,
combine 4 tbsp softened butter,
2 tsp fresh orange zest,
and 1 tbsp toasted
and finely chopped nori seaweed.
Add salt
and pepper to taste and
transfer to a piping bag
with a ¼" tip.

Place a 1' sheet of plastic wrap
on a flat surface
and pipe a horizontal line
of butter mixture.

Roll up the plastic
around the butter into a tight log
and tie off the ends.

Repeat until all the butter is used; freeze the logs.
Remove plastic and slice butter into
1/8"-thick rounds; keep chilled.

In a small bowl,
whisk together 2 tbsp softened butter,
1 tbsp orange juice, and 2 tsp powdered sugar.
Whisk in 1/3 cup flour, then two egg whites;
chill batter.

With an offset spatula,
and using a 1½"-square template as a guide,
evenly spread batter
onto a Silpat*-lined baking sheet
to form the crackers, leaving 1" between.

Sprinkle the top of the crackers
with a few pieces of crispy rice cereal.

Bake in batches at 300°F
for 8 minutes; cool and store
in an airtight container.

Flake 2 tins of olive oil-packed sardines
into large chunks and season with olive oil,
fresh lemon juice, salt, and pepper.

Assemble by topping the rice crackers
with a chunk of sardine
and a slice of seaweed butter.

*Silicone baking mat, available at kitchen and housewares stores.

Herbed Falafel

(Makes 40)

Soak 1¹/₃ cups chickpeas
and ½ cup bulgur wheat separately
in water overnight; strain.

Heat 2 tbsp olive oil in a large skillet
over medium heat
and add ¹/₃ cup diced red onion
and 1 tbsp garlic and cook,
stirring, until translucent.

In a food processor,
combine cooked onion
with chickpeas,
bulgur wheat,
¹/₃ cup chopped parsley,
¼ cup chopped mint,
¼ cup chopped cilantro,
1 tbsp white sesame seeds,
1 tbsp baking powder,
½ tsp cumin,
1 tbsp salt,
1 tsp harissa paste,
and 1 tsp ground
black pepper.

Pulse, occasionally scraping the sides of the bowl
with a spatula, until the chickpeas are finely
minced and everything is well combined.

Roll the mixture into chestnut-size balls
and chill. For dipping sauce,
combine 1 cup thick Greek yogurt
with 2 tbsp harissa paste.

When ready to serve,
deep-fry balls in 350° F vegetable oil
until browned and crispy,
and serve with yogurt sauce.

Pan con Tomate

(Makes 20)

Bring a pot of water to a boil
and place a bowl of ice water on the side.
Core and score the bottoms of 4 Roma
or heirloom tomatoes, boil 1 minute,
then chill in ice water.

Peel tomatoes, cut in quarters,
and trim away seeds.
Dice the flesh and toss with 4 tbsp crème
fraîche, 2 tbsp chopped basil,
and olive oil,
salt, and pepper to taste.

Cut a baguette into ¼" slices,
place on a baking sheet, drizzle with olive oil,
and toast in a 350° F oven until golden brown.

Rub one side of each toast
with a clove of peeled garlic,
top with tomato mixture,
and garnish with basil leaves.

Turkish Lamb
Meatballs with
Tomato Chutney (Makes approximately 30)

In a large bowl,
    combine 1 lb ground lamb,
                8 oz ground beef,
        1/3 cup olive oil,
        ¾ cup dry bread crumbs,
        ¼ cup each minced onion and carrot,
    3 cloves minced garlic,
1 tbsp fresh grated ginger,
        1 egg,
    1 tbsp each chopped cilantro and mint,
and 1½ tbsp Turkish spice mix*.
        Mix well by hand and roll
into 1"-diameter balls.

In a large skillet,
heat a thin layer of olive oil over medium-high heat
and brown meatballs on all sides.

Add 2 tsp Turkish spice

and cook, stirring, until toasty;

remove meatballs, reserving fat.

Add ½ cup chopped onion
and 4 minced garlic cloves
to reserved fat in skillet.
Cook, stirring frequently,
until soft but not colored.

Add 2 tbsp harissa paste
and a 14½ oz can
small-diced tomatoes with juice;
simmer for 15 minutes.

Return meatballs to tomato mixture in
skillet and simmer together, stirring
occasionally, another 15 minutes.

Garnish with fresh chopped cilantro;

serve warm, with skewers.

*See Supplemental Recipes, or use store-bought spice mix.

Essential
Bar Tools

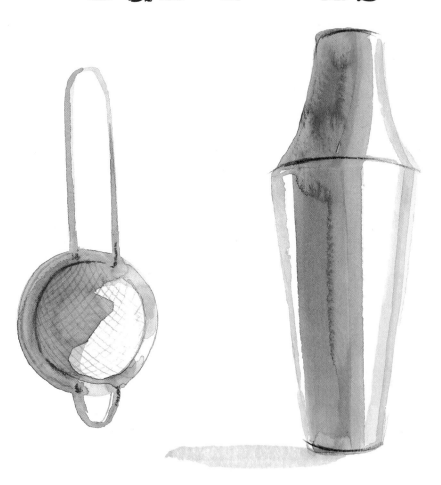

The tools needed to make a good cocktail are:

2 oz / 1 oz double-sided measuring jigger

1 ½ oz / ¾ oz double-sided
measuring jigger

1 oz / ½ oz double-sided
measuring jigger

1 muddler

1 hawthorn strainer

1 bar spoon

1 shaker (2 parts)

1 channel knife

1 Yarai mixing glass

teaspoon (for ¼ oz measure)

Glossary

Candied fennel seeds
Lovely multicolored sweets savored after an Indian meal. The combination of the anise-tasting fennel seed, menthol, and candy coating refreshes the mouth after a rich meal and aids digestion.

Curry leaves
Originally from southern India, mostly used in Indian cuisine and in curry spice mix; the leaves bring a toasted and grilled flavor.

Indonesian cubeb pepper, or tailed pepper
Dried berries similar in appearance to black peppercorns, but with a tiny stalk or tail attached. In India, cubeb paste was used as a mouthwash, and dried cubebs were taken internally for oral and dental diseases, loss of voice, fevers, and cough. Harvested in Java and other Indonesian islands, and also some African countries.

Kaffir lime leaves
Also known as makrut lime leaves, a culinary gift from Southeast Asia. They impart a citrusy, floral aroma.

Supplemental Recipes

Cinnamon syrup
Bring to a boil 500 grams (2 cups) of water with 500 grams (2 rounded cups) of white sugar and 15 cinnamon sticks. Let steep in the refrigerator for a day, then strain mixture into a clean, sealed container. Can be kept refrigerated for up to 3 weeks.

Cucumber juice
Peel a whole cucumber (the skin is bitter) and juice it in a juice extractor.

Earl Grey tea infused bourbon
Steep 3 Earl Grey tea bags in 1 liter of bourbon, covered, for 4 hours at room temperature. Strain the bourbon back into its original bottle, and store, sealed, at room temperature.

Ginger beer (inspired by Dale DeGroff's recipe)

2½ pounds ginger root, peeled and roughly chopped
4 limes
¾ cup light brown sugar
In a large pot, bring 2 gallons of water to a boil, then remove from flame. While the water is heating, pulse ginger with a few drops of hot water in a food processor until minced, and add to the boiled water. With a spoon, remove the lime flesh and juice, and drop it into the water along with the ginger peels. Add sugar, stir until dissolved, and let steep, covered, for 1 hour. Strain through a fine chinois or cheesecloth, pour into nonplastic containers, let cool, then refrigerate. Can be kept refrigerated for a few weeks, but is best fresh; the ginger flavor diminishes over time. When ready to serve, pour into a soda siphon.

Ginger juice

Peel a fresh ginger root, and juice it with a juice extractor.

Grissini dough

For use with the Black Olive Grissini recipe on page 58.
In a medium-size mixing bowl, whisk together 1 lb 00 pasta flour and 2 tsp fine sea salt; form a well in the center and set aside. In a small bowl, whisk together 1 cup warm water, 1 tbsp plus 1 tsp sugar, and 1 tbsp active dry yeast; rest 10 minutes, allowing it to foam. Add liquid to the well in the bowl of flour with ½ cup plus 1 tbsp extra virgin olive oil. Starting in the center, mix with a spoon, gradually pulling the flour into the liquid, then switch to mixing with your hands. Once it comes together, knead on the countertop for 5 minutes until smooth. Wrap in plastic and rest at room temperature 1 hour. Use immediately or store in refrigerator up to 2 days.

Hollow ice ball

Clean the inside of a party balloon, fill it with filtered water to make a ball large enough to fit the cocktail glass, and tie it closed. Suspend balloon by its knot from a grid and place in freezer, with nothing touching it so it keeps its shape. Freeze until outer shell is frozen, about an hour and a half, depending on freezer and size of ice ball. Remove balloon, make a hole in semi-frozen ice ball with a hot utensil, and pour out unfrozen water from center. Keep hollow ice ball in freezer until ready to serve, then use a funnel to fill.

Jalapeño juice	Remove the stem, and juice the whole pepper with a juice extractor.
Lapsang souchong tea infused cognac	Steep 3 lapsang souchong tea bags in 1 liter of cognac, covered, for 4 hours at room temperature. Strain the cognac back into its original bottle, and store, sealed, at room temperature.
Oolong tea infused cachaça	Steep 2 bags of coconut oolong tea and 10 kaffir lime leaves in 1 liter of cachaça, covered, for 4 hours at room temperature. Double strain cachaça back into its original bottle, and store, sealed, at room temperature.
Simple syrup	Bring to a boil 1000 grams (4 cups) of water with 900 grams (4 cups) of white sugar. Let cool, and pour into a clean, sealed container. Can be kept refrigerated for up to 3 weeks.
Spice syrup	Bring to a boil 500 grams (2 cups) of water with 500 grams (2 rounded cups) of white sugar, 8 cinnamon sticks, 8 cloves, and half a ground nutmeg. Let steep in the refrigerator for a day, then strain mixture into a clean, sealed container. Can be kept refrigerated for up to 3 weeks.
Turkish spice mix	*For use with the Turkish Lamb Meatballs recipe on page 68.* In a small, dry skillet, combine ¼ of a crushed cinnamon stick, 1 tbsp cumin seeds, 2 tsp fennel seeds, 2 tsp coriander seeds, 2 cloves, and 2 tsp black peppercorns. Over medium heat, stir occasionally until mixture smells well toasted but not burned. Transfer to a spice grinder and blend to a powder. Combine with 2 tsp smoked paprika and 1 tbsp fine sea salt. Store in a dry, sealed container.

Resources

For bitters, barware, and accessories, visit Cocktail Kingdom, cocktailkingdom.com.
Spherical ice mold set available from the MoMA Store, momastore.org.
Special spice blends available from La Boîte à Épice, laboitenyc.com.

Acknowledgments

I would like to thank the countless New York City bartenders who have inspired me and whose creativity has raised modern mixology to such a distinguished level; Lior Lev Sercarz at La Boîte à Épice; Fernando Castellon, mixologist at Bar Expertise (www.barexpertise.com); Karlyn Monroe, Erin Williams, and the entire Cointreau team; Maximilian Riedel and Elizabeth Arout at Riedel; Francesco Lafranconi, director of mixology at Southern Wine and Spirits; the Assouline team, for their kindness, patience, and professionalism; Gilles Bensabeur at St-Germain Elderflower Liqueur; Edixon Caridad at Santa Teresa Rum; Lizzie da Trindade-Asher at La Diablada Pisco; Dave Hughes at Haus Alpenz; and all the liquor companies I have worked with, for bringing such a diversity of quality spirits to NYC.

At Daniel, special thanks go to Daniel Boulud, first and foremost, for trusting me and giving me the opportunity to do this cocktail book; pastry chef Dominique Ansel, for always being an inspiration; executive chef Jean François Bruel; chef de cuisine Eddy Leroux; Pierre Siue, general manager, who is always a step ahead; recipe editor AJ Schaller, for her wonderful writing and testing; and all the team at Daniel for their support, especially sommelier Caleb Ganzer, our former bartenders Susan Chung and Brian O'Neil, and Arnaud Dissais and all the bartenders who have worked with me and brought their contributions to the cocktail program. I have learned so much from each of you. Above all, thanks to my parents, Aline and Yves Herit, for always believing in me, and to my wife, Sarah Green-Herit, for her constant encouragement and support.

Xavier Herit